how to
Mind
Map®

TONY BUZAN

how to
Mind
Map®

Thorsons

Thorsons
An Imprint of HarperCollins*Publishers*
77–85 Fulham Palace Road,
Hammersmith, London W6 8JB

The Thorsons website address is: www.thorsons.com

and *Thorsons* are trademarks of
HarperCollins*Publishers* Limited

First published by Thorsons 2002

10 9 8 7 6 5 4 3 2 1

A catalogue record of this book is
available from the British Library

ISBN 0-00-714684-1 PB
ISBN 0-00-715373-2 HB

Printed and bound in Great Britain by
Martins The Printers Limited, Berwick upon Tweed

Dedication

This book is dedicated to the human brain
and its incredible powers of Imagination and
Association, which are unleashed by the
magic of Mind Maps®.

Contents

Chapter Three:
Your Daily Life Made More Successful
with Mind Maps 37

List of Mind Maps

Acknowledgements

I would like to thank especially the following people who have been especially significant in the development of Mind Maps and in their growing global acceptance: my dear friend Sean Adam who in 1986 predicted that within 20 years Mind Maps would be *the* Global Thinking Tool and who encouraged me to make sure that it was!; my Personal Assistant Lesley Bias without whose "burning fingers" you would not be reading this book!; Alan Burton our Mind Map artist who so brilliantly brings the ideas to life; my Buzan Licensed Instructors (BLIs) and Master Trainers who have been spreading the "Mind Map News" throughout the five continents and to all corners of the globe; my brother Professor Barry Buzan whose constant support and encouragement have increased the speed at which Mind Maps have spread around the world; my Mum Jean Buzan for helping me to develop my own thinking abilities and for her excellent editing of my books; Michael J. Gelb, Mind Map supporter and colleague; the artist Lorraine Gill who proved to me that I and everybody in the world could both draw and was a natural artist; HSH Prince Philipp of Liechtenstein, the first Company Chairman to both realize the importance of Mind Maps and to commit to giving everybody in his company, the Liechtenstein Global Trust, the opportunity to benefit from them; Vanda North the founder of The Buzan Centers whose dedication to making Mind Maps known and available throughout the world has been astonishing and astonishingly successful; Caroline Shott my Literary Manager whose brilliant idea this book was and who inspired the stunning new portfolio of Thorsons books of which this book is a part; especial thanks to my dear friend and Editor-in-Chief Carole Tonkinson for her constant support and enthusiasm for Mind Maps. Continuing thanks

How to Mind Map

to my extraordinary support team at Thorsons who have now become family. Each one of the following has excelled in their given field and helped to make this book a success: Commissioning Editor Helen Evans, Senior Project Editor Kate Latham, Senior Designer Jacqui Caulton, Design Manager Jo Ridgeway, Senior Marketing Manager Jo Lal and Publicity Director Megan Slyfield.

A Letter to My Readers

Let me tell you the story of how Mind Maps and *How to Mind Map* came into being.

As a young child I had loved the idea of taking notes and of learning. By the time I was a teenager my thinking was already getting into a mess, and I began to hate anything to do with study, especially note-taking. I began to notice the extraordinary paradox that the more notes I took the **worse** my studies and memory became. In an effort to improve matters I began to underline key words and ideas in red and to put important things in boxes. Magically, my memory began to improve.

In my first year of university, I was still struggling. It was then that I became fascinated by the Greeks, for I learned that they had developed memory systems that enabled them to recall perfectly hundreds and thousands of facts. The Greek memory systems were based on Imagination and Association, which I noticed to my amusement and concern were absent from my own notes!

I then began to notice that everyone around me was taking the same kind of crowded, one-color and monotonous notes as I was. None of us was using the principles of Imagination and Association—we were all in the same sinking boat!

I suddenly realized that in my head and the collective "global brain," there was a gigantic log-jam that needed a new note-taking and thinking tool to unblock it.

I set out in search of a thinking tool that would give us the freedom to think and the freedom to think in the way we were **designed** to think.

I began to study every subject I could, especially psychology. In psychology I discovered that there were two main things important to the brain during learning: Association and Imagination. Similar to the Greeks! By now I was becoming fascinated by my brain and what I realized were its power and potential. The power and potential were both much greater than I had thought. I began to focus on memory, note-taking and creativity, as it seemed that the answer to my quest would lie with them.

I quickly discovered that most of the great thinkers, especially Leonardo da Vinci, used pictures, codes and connecting lines in their notes. They "doodled" and thus made their notes come alive.

During all these explorations, I would often wander in nature, where I found it much easier to think, imagine and dream. It began to dawn on me that, as we are part of nature, our thinking and note-making must relate to nature and must reflect nature; we must mirror the universal laws of nature in our own functioning!

There was only one possible solution to my dilemma. The thinking tool had to apply to the full range of human daily activities, and had to be based on the way the brain naturally wants to work. I needed something that reflected the processes of nature and how our brains naturally work rather than something that put us in a mental strait-jacket by forcing us to work against our natural design. What emerged was a star-like, simple, and beautiful tool that did reflect the natural creativity and radiance of our thinking processes.

The first Mind Map was born!

The British Broadcasting Corporation (BBC) heard about this new discovery and about its remarkable effect on children. As a result they asked me to do a half-an-hour television program on Mind Maps.

At the meeting to discuss the content of the program, I Mind Mapped the brain-storming session. Looking at the growing Mind Map, the Head of BBC Further Education exclaimed: "There's more than one program here. There are at least ten!" Within a year the "Use Your Head" ten-part television series and accompanying book were launched. The Mind Map had created its own future!

Since then I have devoted my time to lecturing and teaching about the theory and application of Mind Maps. Having struggled through my student days, I was determined that everyone should have the benefit of this liberating thinking tool.

As part of this determination to make Mind Maps accessible to everyone, I have written *How to Mind Map*. It will introduce you to what a Mind Map is, how Mind Maps work, the many ways in which Mind Maps can help you and how you can use them.

How to Mind Map will guide you through the simple process of building up a Mind Map from the start. You will quickly be inspired by what you can achieve, how creative you can be and how Mind Maps will bring you immediate practical help in your daily life.

Mind Maps wonderfully and dramatically changed my life for the better. I know that they will do the same for you.

Prepare to be amazed—by yourself!

How to Mind Map

introducing the

Mind Map®!

In this chapter I will answer the following questions:

- Just What *Is* a Mind Map?

- What Do You Need to Make a Mind Map?

- How Can Mind Maps Help You?

Just What *Is* a Mind Map®?

A Mind Map is the ultimate organizational thinking tool. And it is so simple!

The very basic Mind Map below is a plan for today. Each of the branches emanating from the central image relate to different things that need to be done today, for example, calling a plumber, or doing the grocery shopping.

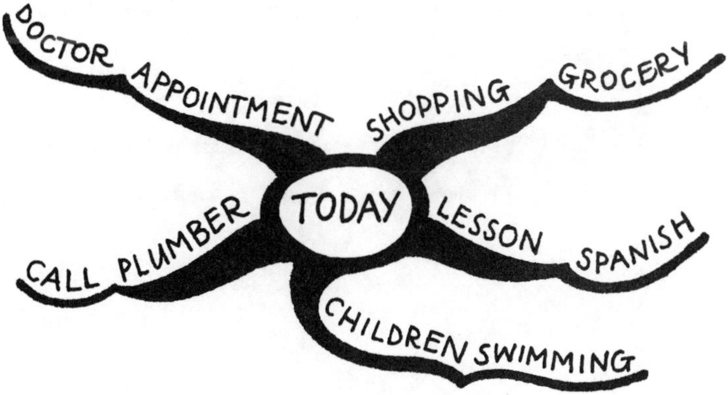
TODAY
DOCTOR APPOINTMENT
SHOPPING GROCERY
LESSON SPANISH
CALL PLUMBER
CHILDREN SWIMMING

A Mind Map is the easiest way to put information *into* your brain and to take information *out* of your brain—it's a creative and effective means of note-taking that literally

"maps out"

your thoughts.

How to Mind Map

All Mind Maps have some things in common. They all use color. They all have a natural structure that radiates from the center. And they all use lines, symbols, words and images according to a set of simple, basic, natural and brain-friendly rules. With a Mind Map, a long list of boring information can be turned into a colorful, memorable, highly organized diagram that works in line with your brain's natural way of doing things.

You can usefully compare Mind Maps to maps of a city. The center of your Mind Map is like the center of the city, and represents your most important idea; the main roads leading from the center represent the main thoughts in your thinking process; the secondary roads or branches represent your secondary thoughts, and so on. Special images or shapes can represent sights of interest or particularly interesting ideas.

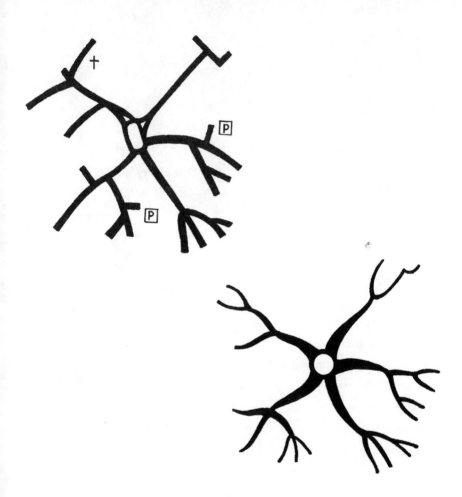

Just like a road map, a Mind Map will:

- Give an overview of a large subject or area.
- Enable you to plan routes or to make choices, and will let you know where you are going and where you have been.
- Gather together large amounts of data in one place.
- Encourage problem solving by allowing you to see new creative pathways.
- Be enjoyable to look at, read, muse over and remember.

Mind Maps are also brilliant

route-maps

for the memory, allowing you to organize facts and thoughts
in such a way that your brain's natural way of working is
engaged right from the start. This means that remembering
and recalling information later is far easier and more reliable
than when using traditional note-taking techniques.

What Do You Need to Make a Mind Map?

Because Mind Maps are so easy to do and so natural, the ingredients for your "Mind Map Recipe" are very few:

1. Blank unlined paper
2. Colored pens and pencils
3. Your brain
4. Your imagination!

How Can Mind Maps Help You?

Mind Maps can help you in many, **many** ways!
Here are just a few!

Mind Maps can help you to:

- be more creative
- save time
- solve problems
- concentrate
- organize and clarify your thinking
- pass exams with good grades
- remember better
- study faster and more efficiently
- make studying a breeze
- see the "whole picture"
- plan
- communicate
- survive!
- save trees!

Let's compare your

brain

and the

knowledge

in it to a library.

Imagine that your brain is a newly built and empty library waiting to be filled with data and information in the form of books, videos, films, CDs and computer discs.

You are the chief librarian and have to choose first whether you wish to have a small or a large selection. You naturally choose a large selection.

Your second choice is whether to have the information organized or not.

Imagine that you take the second option, **not** to have it organized: you simply order a dumpster of books and electronic media, and have it all piled in a giant heap of information in the middle of your library floor! When somebody comes into your library and asks for a specific book or place where they can find information on a specific topic, you shrug your shoulders and say: "It's somewhere there in the pile, hope you find it—good luck!"

This metaphor describes the state of most people's minds!

Their minds, even though they may—and often do—contain the information they want, are so horribly disorganized that it is impossible for them to retrieve information when they need it. This leads to frustration and a reluctance to take in or handle any new information. After all, what is the point of taking in new information, if you are never going to be able to access the stuff anyway?!

Imagine, on the other hand, that you have a giant library, filled with incredible amounts of information on everything you ever wanted to know. In this new super-library, rather than all this information being piled randomly in the middle of the floor, everything is filed in perfect order, exactly where you want it.

In addition to this, the library has a phenomenal data-retrieval and access system that enables you to find anything you want at the flash of a thought.

An impossible dream? An immediate possibility for you!

Mind Maps *are* that phenomenal data-retrieval and access system for the gigantic library that actually exists in your amazing brain.

Mind Maps help you to learn, organize, and store as much information as you want, and to classify it in natural ways that give you easy and instant access (perfect memory!) to whatever you want.

Mind Maps have an additional strength. You would think that the more information you put into your head, the more stuffed your head would become and the more difficult it would be to get any information out. Mind Maps turn this thought on *its* head!

Why?

Because with Mind Maps each new piece of information you put into your library automatically "hooks on to" all the information already in there. With more of these grappling-hooks-of-memory attaching to any piece of information in your head, the more easy it is for you to "hook out" whatever information you need. With Mind Maps, the more you know and learn, the ***easier*** it is to learn and know more!

In summary, Mind Mapping has a whole range of advantages that help make your life easier and more successful.

It's time for you to start your first one!

chapter two

making a

Mind Map®

- Discovering Your Natural Mind Mapping Ability

- Imagination and Association Game

- Seven Steps to Making a Mind Map

- Creating Your First Mind Map

In this chapter you are going to make your first Mind Map, starting with an Imagination and Association game.

You will graduate from this chapter knowing how to Mind Map and having learned all the ingredients that go into making a great Mind Map.

Discovering Your Natural Mind Mapping Ability

How does a Mind Map work? In the same way your brain works!

And fortunately, although your brain can do the most incredibly complex things, it is based on the most profoundly

simple principles. That is why Mind Maps are easy and fun
to create, because they work with your brain's natural needs
and energy rather than against them.

So what **are** the keys to your brain's functioning?

Quite simply:

imagination

and

association

Doubt it? Then try this game and make your first Mind Map.

Imagination and Association Game

Read the word printed in capital letters below and immediately close your eyes and keep them closed for about 30 seconds and think about it.

FRUIT

When you read the word and then closed your eyes, was all that popped into your mind a little computer printout of the word: F-R-U-I-T?!

Of course not! What your brain probably generated was an image of your favorite single fruit, or a bowl of fruit, or a fruit store, and so on. You probably also saw the colors of different fruits, connected the tastes to appropriate fruits, and similarly "experienced" their aromas. This is because our brains work

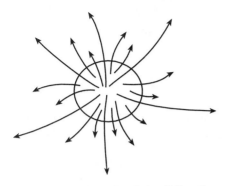

Your brain thinks radiantly in all directions.

with sensory *images* with appropriate links and *associations* radiating from them. Our brains use words to trigger these images and associations. They produce 3-D *pictures* with numerous associations that are especially personal to us.

What *you* have demonstrated with the "Fruit Exercise" is that your brain Mind Maps naturally! And in doing so, you have accomplished even more than you thought, and opened the way for phenomenal improvement in your thinking power. You have learned how your brain actually works!

To get some insight into just how brilliant your brain is and how important Mind Maps are as a method for allowing it to express itself naturally and easily, think again about the "Fruit Exercise" you have just completed: how quickly **did** you get that image of fruit? Most people answer "immediately."

In daily conversation you are accessing "immediately" a constant **stream** of continuing data so easily and elegantly that you don't even notice that your brain is doing something that makers of the world's super-computers can only dream of doing! You already possess the ultimate super-computer. And it's in your head!

It is this amazing "super-computer power" that Mind Maps harness.

Mind Maps are the reflection of your brain's natural, image-filled thinking processes and abilities.

This is how our brains work—

IMAGES

with networks of

ASSOCIATION

This is how Mind Maps work—

IMAGES

with networks of

ASSOCIATION

Seven Steps to Making a Mind Map

1. Start in the **CENTER** of a blank page turned sideways. Why? **Because starting in the center gives your brain freedom to spread out in all directions and to express itself more freely and naturally.**

2. Use an IMAGE or PICTURE for your central idea. Why? **Because an image is worth a thousand words and helps you use your Imagination. A central image is more interesting, keeps you focused, helps you concentrate, and gives your brain more of a buzz!**

3. Use COLORS throughout. Why? **Because colors are as exciting to your brain as are images. Color adds extra vibrancy and life to your Mind Map, adds tremendous energy to your Creative Thinking, and is fun!**

4. CONNECT your MAIN BRANCHES to the central IMAGE and connect your second- and third-level branches to the first and second levels, etc. Why? **Because, as you now know, your brain works by ASSOCIATION. If you connect the branches, you will understand and remember a lot more easily.**

Connecting your main branches also creates and establishes a basic structure or architecture for your thoughts. This is very similar to the way in which in nature a tree has connected branches that radiate from its central trunk. If there were little gaps between the trunk and its main branches or between those main branches and the smaller branches and twigs, nature wouldn't work quite so well! Without connection in your Mind Map, everything (especially your memory and learning!) falls apart. Connect!

5. Make your branches CURVED rather than straight-lined. Why? **Because having nothing but straight lines is *boring* to your brain. Curved, organic branches, like the branches of trees, are far more attractive and riveting to your eye.**

6. Use ONE KEY WORD PER LINE. Why? **Because single key words give your Mind Map more power and flexibility. Each single word or image is like a multiplier, generating its own special array of associations and connections. When you use single key words, each one is freer and therefore better able to spark off new ideas and new thoughts. Phrases or sentences tend to dampen this triggering effect. A Mind Map with more key words in it is like a hand with all the finger joints working. A Mind Map with phrases or sentences is like a hand with all your fingers held in rigid splints!**

7. Use IMAGES throughout. Why? **Because each image, like the central image, is also worth a thousand words. So if you have only 10 images in your Mind Map, it's already the equal of 10,000 words of notes!**

Creating Your First Mind Map

Let's return to the topic of "Fruit" and use your powers of imagination and association to make a Mind Map. There is a sample Mind Map on Plate 1, but try to complete the Mind Map yourself before you look at it.

Level One

First take a sheet of plain paper and some colored pens. Turn the piece of paper on its side, so that it is wider than it is long (landscape rather than portrait). In the center of the page draw an **image** that sums up **"Fruit"** for you. Use the colored pens and be as creative as you like. Now label this image "Fruit."

Level Two

Then, draw some thick branches radiating out from the central "Fruit" image. Use a different color for each. These branches will represent your **main thoughts on** "Fruit." You can add any number of branches when you make a Mind Map, but, for the purposes of this exercise, let's limit the number of branches to five (see illustration opposite).

On each branch, print clearly and in large capital letters the first five single key words that pop into your head when you think of the concept "Fruit."

Basic form to copy for your first Mind Map (Level II)

As you can see, at the moment, your Mind Map is primarily composed of lines and words. So how can we improve it?

We can make it better by adding to it the important brain ingredients of *pictures* and *images* from your **IMAGINATION**. "A picture is worth a thousand words" and therefore saves you a *lot* of time and wasted energy writing down those thousand words in your notes! And it is easier to remember.

Making a Mind Map   **33**

For each of your key words, draw in a picture next to it to represent and reinforce it. Use your colored pens and a little imagination. It doesn't have to be a masterpiece—a Mind Map is not a test of your artistic ability!

Level Three

Now let's use ASSOCIATION to expand this Mind Map on to its next stage. Returning to your Mind Map, take a look at the five key words you have written down on each of the main branches. Do these key words spark off further ideas? For example, if, say, you had written the word "Orange" you might think of color, juice, Florida, Vitamin C, and so on.

Draw further branches coming off each of your key words to accommodate the associations you make. Again, the number of sub-branches you have is totally dependent on the

Basic form for you to copy for your first Mind Map (Level III)

number of ideas you come up with—which may be infinite.
However, for this exercise, draw in three sub-branches.

On these sub-branches do exactly the same as you did in
the first stage of this game: print, clearly, single key words

on these waiting-to-be-filled branches. Use the main word on the branch to trigger your three new key words. Again, remember to use color and images on these sub-branches.

Congratulations! You have just completed your first basic Mind Map. You will notice that even at this early stage your Mind Map is brimming with symbols, codes, lines, words, colors, and images, and is already demonstrating all the basic guidelines you need in order to apply your brain most effectively and enjoyably. For a completed "master example" of this exercise, see Plate 1.)

You are now more than ready to explore the exciting world of Mind Map applications and how they can add quality, effectiveness, and success to your personal, family, professional, and daily life.

your daily life made more successful with

Mind Maps®

- Communication and Presentations Mind Map

- Planning Family Events Mind Map

- Persuading People and Negotiating with Mind Maps

- Romantic Weekend Mind Map

- Telephone Calls Mind Map

- Starting a New Venture Mind Map

- Shopping Mind Map

- How to Reduce a Book to a Single Page Mind Map

Now you have mastered the basics, it is time to introduce you to a range of the most popular and successful applications for Mind Maps in your daily life.

You now know that Mind Maps have many advantages, including saving time, organizing and clarifying your thinking, generating new ideas, keeping track of things, dramatically improving memory and concentration, stimulating more of your brain, allowing you to keep your eye on the "whole picture," and, very importantly, being fun to do!

In this chapter I am going to put all these advantages to work for you.

You will learn how to apply this master thinking technique to a whole range of the most important Life Skills including planning, shopping, studying, note-taking, coming to new realizations and awareness, and making presentations.

Communication and Presentations Mind Map

Being asked to make a speech or presentation is ranked as the number one fear on the planet—higher than the fear of snakes, spiders, rodents, war, disease, violence, and even death!

Because when making a speech or presentation we are both physically and mentally utterly exposed. There is no escaping the inevitable mistakes in front of the audience. Thus the dread.

To deal with this dread, most people spend hours and days preparing written presentations that waste precious time and which often have the opposite effect to that desired.

Because they are written in sentence form, and because we do not speak in this form, they become monotonous and boring. In addition, because you have to keep on looking down at the words, you lose contact with the audience. In further addition, because you have to keep looking back up at the audience you increase the probability that you will lose your place. On top of all this, because you have to hold the pages, you trap your extraordinarily expressive body in an immobile prison, thus losing more than 50% of your communication ability at the start.

Mind Maps to the rescue!

In the same way as you Mind Mapped "Fruit," simply place the topic of the speech in the center of the page, and radiate out the main key images and words you wish to address.

When you have completed the Mind Map, number the central branches in the order in which they are to be presented, and highlight any major points or any major connections between the branches.

You will be delighted to know that for making speeches, the standard rule is one key word or image for one-minute's worth of speech on a topic you know well. Thus for a half-an-hour speech you need only a small Mind Map to complete your task more than successfully.

The advantage of using a Mind Map for presentations, which millions of people in the business world now do, is that it keeps your mind constantly aware of the

"whole picture,"

allows you to add and subtract information as the time for your presentation approaches, and guarantees that you will cover all the major points you wish to address. Your eyes will be able to make much more contact with your audience, your body will be a lot more free, and so will your mind.

Presentation Mind Maps give you that ultimate freedom —the freedom to be yourself. And audiences appreciate

Plate 1: Basic Mind Map® on "Fruit"

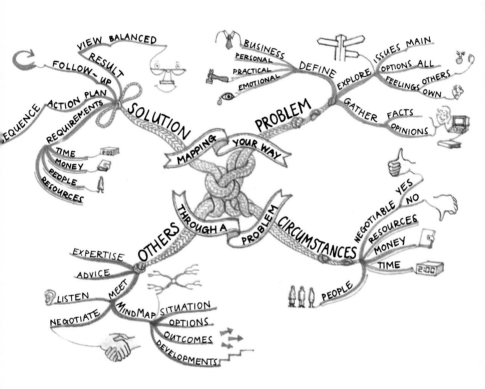

Plate 2: Mind Mapping® Your Way through a Problem

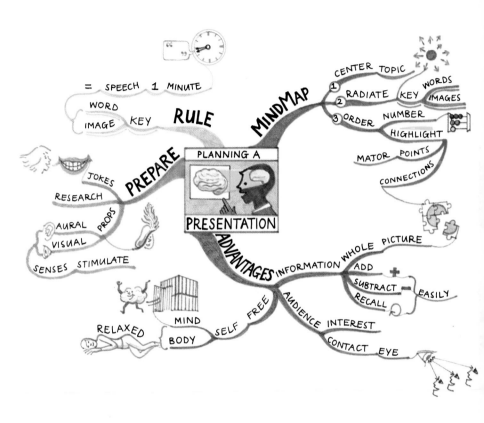

Plate 3: Planning a Presentation Mind Map®

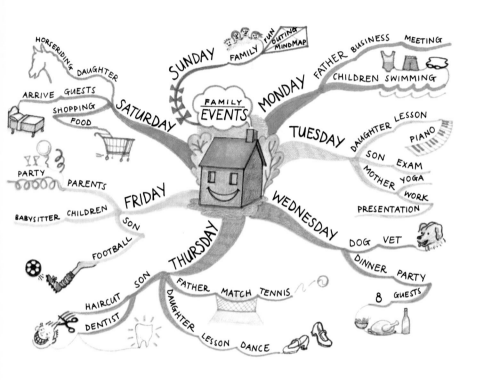

Plate 4: Planning Family Events Mind Map®

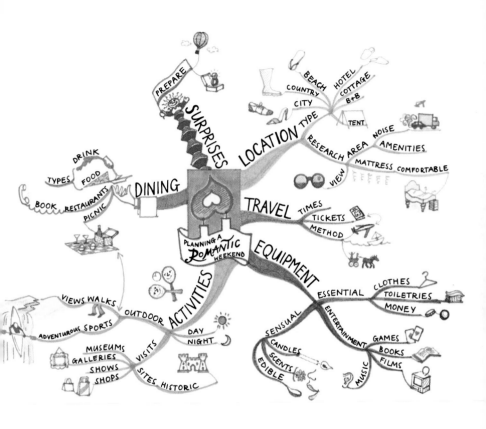

Plate 5: Planning a Romantic Weekend Mind Map®

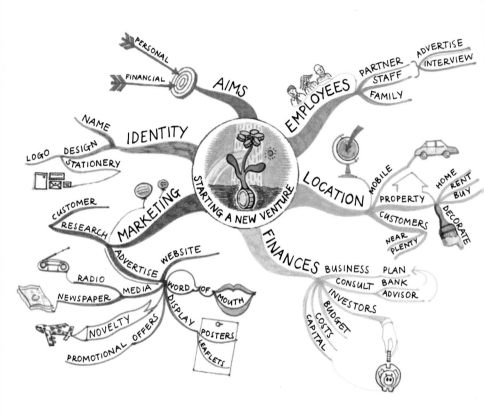

Plate 6: Starting a New Venture

Plate 7: Shopping Mind Map®

Plate 8: Your Ideal Future

nothing more than someone who is doing just that.

For an example of completed Mind Map on this subject, turn to Plate 3.

Planning Family Events Mind Map

A dear friend of mine uses Mind Maps to plan all her family's daily, weekly, annual, and special events.

Her Mind Maps appear in a place, commonly known as the community hub of the family and where they are increasingly to be found: on her fridge door!

She, in her own words, will tell you how she uses them, what for, and what the advantages are.

Before I had heard about Tony and his Mind Maps, I was in chaos! I consider myself a pretty typical twenty-first century woman—I want it all! I am a wife, a mother, I have a career, I like to keep fit and I *love* my social life. Everything has equal importance and I enjoy all the demands and successes. And I certainly don't want to miss out on anything, least of all any of my son's important activities—be they studying for exams, attending a concert, helping him with his art project, or making sure his hair is cut in time for the school photo!

However, I realized that wanting it all meant that I had to be *super* efficient in my organization at home. While packing my briefcase for the following day's meetings, had I remembered to pick up the dry-cleaned suit for my husband's important meeting the next day, or that the dog's appointment with the vet was at 3.00 p.m. at precisely the same time as I had a meeting, so who was going to take him? And which day of the week was it in my son's school schedule? If tomorrow was Wednesday, he needed his football boots and his piano music and would need to be picked up later than usual as he was in the school musical rehearsal and then when he came home he had homework to do before supper, bath and bed! Oh, and my mother was arriving for two days—must make sure the guest bed had clean sheets on and get in more food, and send off the deposit for our vacation or we would lose the reservation! And remember to call Susie to tell her that I can't join her at the yoga class after all because of all of the above.

Most of the time, we somehow muddled through (with frantic phone calls from the school about some vital piece of equipment that had been forgotten and equally frantic calls from my husband reminding me of that important business dinner that yes, I *had* forgotten about). Then I heard about Mind Maps. I couldn't think what on earth these could possibly be, but was sold on the idea that on one piece of paper I could *map* out our daily or weekly diary so that all of us knew just exactly what the other was doing and what was needed. This has quite simply *transformed* my life! I now have a Mind Map on our fridge door and can *visually* see what the week ahead holds. It goes up at the weekend and we all do it together and add to it as the week progresses. I don't think my life has ever run so efficiently.

What my friend has demonstrated is that a Mind Map is a wonderful way to note down, in an attractive and organized way, everything you have to do. You can either have one overall Mind Map or a series of mini-Mind Maps that cover the areas of your future activities. These Mind Maps will give you a good degree of control over your future, and will help you plan far more easily and effectively.

For an example of one of her Mind Maps see Plate 4.

Persuading People and Negotiating with Mind Maps

Persuading other people to see things from our point of view is necessary for survival.

In every walk of life and on a daily basis, we are all involved in persuading people. Whether it be deciding on where to go on vacation, bargaining for a better deal, attempting to sell something, or even applying for a job, the result depends on our ability to

persuade.

In these communications you need to be prepared, and a Mind Map is an excellent preparation tool.

Before entering the "persuasion zone", Mind Map out the *entire* situation, including as your main branches the big goals you have in the situation. Consider the arguments you want to put forward, and note them down in key words and images. You could, for example, use a Mind Map to argue for a raise. You could use the Mind Map to map out all the reasons you deserve more money, taking into account not just your strengths but your weaknesses, in order to pre-empt any objections. You could also use the Mind Map to highlight any particular successes you have had in your present role.

It is also a good idea to include other people's points of views in your Mind Map. When you do this, it gives you a much better overall picture, and allows you to make your points in a spirit of mutual co-operation rather than one of mutual combat!

Mind Maps are especially useful when it comes to negotiating contracts. Getting that all-important "whole picture" and proper perspective is far easier if you use a Mind Map. A Mind Map also helps you add as much detail as necessary without getting lost, because words, colors, symbols, and other Mind Mapping techniques concentrate the information while at the same time organizing it effectively for you.

Color codes

are especially useful. They can highlight areas that are negotiable, non-negotiable, or neutral while the contract is being negotiated. This allows you to concentrate on what is important and not waste time and energy on the irrelevant.

The more contract negotiations get bogged down, the more the Mind Map comes to the rescue. It enables you to see the "whole picture" all the time and that you see relationships that might otherwise be invisible.

One lawyer, who was negotiating a long and complex case, used Mind Maps to keep track of everything over a period of six months. His memory of and grasp of the case was so immense, complex, and complete that his offices were raided by the opposition looking for the secret electronic equipment they thought he must be smuggling into court to give him such perfect control of the case!

Romantic Weekend Mind Map

Planning a romantic weekend can cause a lot of anxiety and stress, because it is *so* important that such events are wonderfully successful. As with any other form of planning, if any vital ingredient is missing or forgotten, the whole event could be a catastrophe. This is where Mind Maps can come to the rescue again!

With your Romantic Weekend Mind Map you will radiate, from a suitably romantic central image, the main branches of the things you need to consider.

These will include location, travel, activities, food, drinks, equipment (including clothes, toiletries, books, and games), and special surprises, etc.

Perhaps the main advantage of the Mind Map for planning the romantic weekend is that it gives a much greater probability that the weekend will be a success, and simultaneously gives you more confidence and less stress.

The confident and relaxed individual is a much more attractive romantic partner!

For an example of a completed Mind Map on this subject, turn to Plate 5.

Telephone Calls Mind Map

Many people make notes during important telephone calls. Business calls, for example, can be extremely complicated and it is easy to miss information if you are not adequately prepared. Similarly, if you are planning a vacation, you may need to jot down details of your itinerary. A Mind Map is *ideal* for this purpose.

Begin with the central image that summarizes either the topic of the conversation or the essence of the person with whom you are talking. Your first main branch will include the person's name and the date. You print each main subject on a branch radiating from the center, adding details using single key words, codes, and images printed on the smaller branches.

As the conversation progresses, the information goes on the page in a way that helps your brain ORGANIZE, REMEMBER, COMPARE, and CONNECT very quickly. When the subject changes, add another branch using key images, codes, and words on the line as before. When the conversation goes back to an early subject, simply go back to the appropriate branch and add the new information.

The telephone conversation can regularly dance from topic to topic, often returning to particular points again and again. With the Mind Map, this is easy to handle because the information always ends up where it belongs. Normal notes simply record, chronologically (not truly logically) the flow of data. This means that the key information gets scattered and lost. You will often find that the information coming out of your telephone call Mind

Map is a lot more organized than the information that originally came in on the telephone!

In telephone call Mind Maps, color adds another useful dimension. You might use red for what you have to act on right away and blue for things you can deal with later.

Pre-drawing the branches for calls *you* initiate is a good way to keep things on track. This will allow the branchés and key words and images to remind you of both what the conversation is about and your goals. People who use Mind Maps get more information across in less time. They are also much more organized and focused because they have a picture of what they want to talk about in front of them.

When you do pre-draw your Mind Maps in this way, it will avoid the incredibly frustrating experience of having to telephone people back because you have "just remembered" (*after* you have hung up!) a vitally important topic that you forgot to mention.

Telephone call Mind Maps save you time, save you embarrassment and save you money!

Starting a New Venture

As you have seen so far, Mind Maps are a fantastic planning tool. They enable you to see the "whole picture" and ensure that nothing is left to chance. What better way, then, to plan a new venture?

Perhaps you are thinking of starting up your own business, like a store or a company. Or perhaps you want to do something on a smaller scale, like starting up a babysitting service or a social club. Whatever your idea, Mind Maps can help you plan smarter and be more successful.

There are so many things to consider when you are starting up a new venture. It can be a really daunting task. However, if you use a Mind Map you can make sure you have thought everything through carefully first. For example, where will you locate your business? Do you need your own premises or can you work from home? And what about staff? Do you need to employ other people or can you manage alone? How will you finance your venture? Will it take a lot of start-up capital? Do you need to borrow money? All of these issues can be plotted out on your Mind Map, using the key words for each of the main things you have to consider. This will allow you to see problems *before* they arise, and take the necessary steps to avoid them.

As your venture develops, you can use your Mind Map as a constant point of reference to check that things stay on track. For example, very often your finances and cash flow take up so much time and importance that it is easy to forget all the brilliant marketing ideas you had for making money in the first place (ironically, it is these very marketing initiatives that could increase your revenue). But if you refer to your Mind Map on a regular basis, you will not forget any of your initial ideas, and you will be able to implement them when the time is right.

With a Mind Map at your side, you are giving your new venture a

head start

to

success.

For an example of a completed Mind Map on this topic, turn to Plate 6.

Shopping Mind Map

Mind Maps are a wonderful shopping aid. They guarantee that you remember everything you wish to buy, and streamline the entire process. They also feed your brain with a constant diet of whole-brain stimulation as you use the Mind Map to remind you while you shop.

No more the infuriating confetti of random scraps of paper, which fracture your thinking, stress your mind with uncertainty, and as often as not get lost! You could even use a Mind Map to plan out all your shopping when faced with buying gifts for Christmas or other special occasions.

First, draw a central image to remind you of your shopping. Then use each of the main branches to think about each person for whom you are buying. Write their names as key words and draw in some sub-branches on which to put their details. For instance, what are their hobbies, their likes and their dislikes? This will help you decide what gifts would be most suitable.

You can even use the Mind Map to work out the most efficient route for your shopping trip and the best stores for each present. Then, when you actually go out, you can take your Mind Map with you for reference to make sure you remember everything.

Use a Mind Map to shop, and your shopping planning will be faster and more efficient, you will buy everything you wished to buy, you will rid yourself of the nagging doubt that you have forgotten something, and you will never have to make those unnecessary return trips to pick up those things you forgot! (See Plate 7 for a Mind Map on this topic.)

How to Reduce a Book to a Single Page Mind Map

Mind Mapping a book is easy. In fact books are **made** to be Mind Mapped! This can be invaluable for study. Mind Maps enable you to get to grips with the subject before you start, as well as providing a fantastic study aid to which you can refer.

To reduce a book to a single page, first scan through the book, checking for the main divisions and chapter headings. These will give you the main branches of your Mind Map, which can radiate from your central image. The central image will either be one that summarizes the topic of the book or an illustration of the book itself.

With this master structure in place, you can fill in the details as you go, even though you are not always reading "in the right order."

The Mind Map, because it is a "self-organizing system," will present to you the developing overview of the work, increasing your **understanding** and **comprehension**, making your study and learning faster and more enjoyable, and vastly improving your memory.

When you review a Mind Map of a book, it is like looking at a photograph album where you immediately remember vast arrays of information with the trigger of each of those "thousand words" pictures.

Novels are easy to Mind Map. With a novel the chapter headings, if there are any, will probably not make the best main branches. Something else, however, will!

All novels are made up of a number of major component parts, which allow you to condense an entire book onto a single page. These main elements are:

Plot—the structure of events

Characters—their type and development

Setting—the places and times where the events of the novel take place

Language—its general level, the type of vocabulary and its rhythm

Imagery—the kind of images the author provides for your imagination

Themes—the kind of ideas with which the novel deals, including such common themes as love, power, money, religion, etc

Symbolism—where the author substitutes one thing to mean another—for example flowers for love, thunderstorms for anger, calm seas for peace, etc

Philosophy—some books present a point of view in order to challenge the way we think

Genre—novels can be categorized under different headings, for instance, political, adventure, mystery, detective, historical, etc

When you Mind Map a novel in this way, you will never again get confused about which character is which, what time is when or what is actually going on! The Mind Map will be like a beacon for you, lighting your way as you progress, and giving you a far richer, deeper and more complete understanding and appreciation of whatever you read.

If you are studying or planning to take further education courses in *any* subject, book Mind Maps are the ideal way to get that "A!"

Computer Mind Maps

Computers can be helpful when you Mind Map! Although
it is still your brain that comes up with all the ideas, the
latest software can allow you to draw a Mind Map on your
screen. The advantages of this are obvious. You can save
your Mind Maps in a file and then transmit this information
to others. Computer Mind Maps allow you to store vast
amounts of data in Mind Map form, to cross-reference that
data, to shift branches around from one part of the Mind
Map to another, to rearrange entire Mind Maps in light
of new information, and to hold global conferences.

Many companies are now using computer Mind Maps for
storing and sharing information and for keeping track of
projects. Use them in conjunction with handmade Mind
Maps—the combination is explosive!

As you have seen, Mind Maps have **many** and very varied uses.

In the chapter that follows, I will introduce you to Mind Maps as a super-tool for improving your creativity and ability to generate thoughts. Firstly because creativity is such a vital ingredient in our modern lives, and secondly because using Mind Maps creatively reveals a fact about your brain and its potential that will amaze and delight you.

making the most of your creativity with

Mind Maps®

- Unleasing Your Amazing Creative Power with Mind Maps

- Linear Note-taking and Its Problems

- The Worldwide Web in Your Head and Its Creative Power

- The Great Creative Geniuses and Note-taking

This chapter will explore how Mind Maps work through the brain principles of Imagination and Association to maximize your creativity.

Unleashing Your Amazing Creative Power with Mind Maps

Do you feel you are creative?

In this chapter Mind Maps will show you not only that you *are*, but that you are ***amazingly*** creative. To do this, let's go back to the exercise in Chapter 2, on "Fruit". Look back at your own Mind Map or use the sample Mind Map on "Fruit" on Plate 1. There are five main branches radiating from the central image, with three further "twigs" coming off each branch, for a third **level of Association**. By using your imaginative, associative brain, you added key words or images to those branches. This may seem simple, but what your brain did was actually something quite profound. You took a single concept, "Fruit", and radiated from it five key ideas. Thus you multiplied your first creative output by five— that's a 500% increase in creative output.

Next you took your five new, freshly created ideas, and from each of them you created three more new ideas. Another threefold or 300% increase! In no time at all, you started from one idea, and created 15 new ones; a 1,500% increase!

Now ask yourself: "Could I create another five words/ideas from each of the 15 words that radiate from the original key five?" Of course you could! That's another 75 ideas created!

Could you add another five from each of those? Again, of course you could—another 375 ideas! ***That's 37,500% more ideas than when you started!*** Could you keep going to the next level? And the next? And the next and the next? Of course you could! And for how long? Forever! Generating how many ideas? **An *infinite* number!**

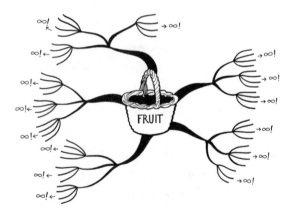

Mind Maps demonstrate that you have ∞ creative abilites.

This new knowledge has immediate applications. You can use it to give you the confidence that you will **always** be able to find an appropriate word, that you will **always** be able to find a solution for a problem; that you will **always** be able to come up with creative ideas; that your natural ability to link and connect will **always** help you with any thinking situation; and that you will **always** now know that you are smarter than you think!

Unconsciously, you have already been demonstrating this infinite creative capacity all your life. It's called procrastination! Just think of the incredible creativity, the amazing number of original ideas, that you generate every day when you think of new reasons (excuses!) for **not** sorting that cupboard, studying that book, doing that unpleasant or boring job … infinite creativity!

When you have generated many creative ideas you can go back, using your mighty association power, and look for links and connections that will generate new super-ideas that will solve your problems, help you make decisions, and help you come up with those new inventions that will make you your fortune!

This infinite association power allows you to generate as many ideas as you want in any creative area. The advantage of this is like the lottery: the more numbers you have, the higher the chance that you will win (come up with the "winning" idea!).

Mind Maps are therefore the best way to express your brain's infinite creative potential. We suddenly see why so many people have problems when they try to use standard linear notes to help them think. Those who Mind Map do not have such problems.

Linear Note-taking and Its Problems

How were you taught to take notes and, indeed, how do you still make them?

If you are like 99.9% of the world's population, you will have been taught, as I was, to make notes that use words, lines, numbers, logic, and sequence.

These are pretty powerful tools.

The only problem is that they are not a complete set. They represent your brain's "left-brain" skills and do not include **any** of your "right-brain" skills, which enable us to comprehend rhythm, color, and space, and to daydream.

In other words, you and I were taught to use only half, or 50%, of our brain's mighty tool-kit. We were, literally, trained to be half-wits!

It's much the same as if I asked you to run 100 meters so that we could check your running efficiency. I give you two trials. In the first one you are allowed to use 100% of your body. You'll probably score in the 90–100% range for efficiency.

In the second trial I allow you 50% of your physical apparatus by tying your right foot up behind your back to your right hand. Once again I ask you to run 100 meters. The result? Flat on your face in the first centimeter! Efficiency comfortably less than zero, because you may well damage yourself in the process!

It's the same with using only "one side" of your brain. Our

traditional notes, in addition to using an incomplete set of tools, have another major weakness.

Students around the world are taught to take notes in blue or black ink or in pencil. In my own school it was even more specific—we had to use only blue-black ink and it had to be of a particular brand. If we dared to use blue or black, we were punished by having to do reams of *lines*! What is the disadvantage of this mono-color note-taking approach?

Think about it: a single color, to your brain, is a ***mono***(single)***tone*** of color.

What word do we get when we combine the concepts of ***mono*** and ***tone***?

Monotone!

And if something is a monotone, it is, by definition, monotonous!

And what do we call something that is particularly monotonous?

Boring!

And what does *your* brain do when it is bored? It tunes out, turns off, drifts, daydreams, and falls asleep.

And it doesn't matter whether you are an English-speaker making notes from left to right, whether you are writing in Hebrew or Arabic making notes from right to left, or Chinese making notes vertically—to the human brain it's all the same, it goes to sleep!

So we conclude that 99.9% of the world's educated, literate, and graduate population is making notes for the vital purposes of creativity, memory, planning, organization, thinking, and communication that are specifically designed to tune them out, turn them off, and send them to sleep!

It is sadly ironic that with this traditional note-taking system, very often the more notes you take, the more complicated simple things begin to seem.

The lines of our traditional notes are like the bars of prison cells in which the infinite creative thinking capability of our brains are incarcerated for life—unless we free them with Mind Maps.

In a very real sense, these sentences that form the prison bars of our brains' prison cells are Prison Sentences!!

Linear notes, by their very nature and structure, train you to become less and less creative. Mind Maps, on the other hand, by using the full power of your imagination and all your left-/right-brain thinking tools, allow you to tap an infinite source of creativity.

The Worldwide Web in Your Head and Its Creative Power

The Worldwide Web is credited with enabling a massive surge of worldwide creativity. In addition we use the Web for accessing information, for communicating, for storing knowledge, and for having fun.

As you are probably beginning to realize, your brain has its own internal Worldwide Web! In fact, your brain is organized much like the Worldwide Web, except that your brain has many advantages:

- It has far superior equipment.
- It is much faster at accessing information.
- It can generate its own information much more rapidly and expansively.
- It contains many more patterns of thought—if you compared the total network of the Worldwide Web with the potential patterns inside your single brain, it would be like comparing a garden pea to a planet!

Mind Maps reflect this internal web, acting as a conduit between your personal universe and the outside universe. The great geniuses, as you will soon discover, understood this.

The Great Creative Geniuses and Note-Taking

As a Mind Mapper, you will begin to facilitate the same thought processes that were used by the greatest creative thinkers in history! Both Leonardo da Vinci and Einstein used their imaginations fully. It was Einstein who said:

"Imagination is more important than knowledge."

And Einstein was correct!

Leonardo da Vinci, in 2000 voted The Brain of the Millennium, is the perfect example of the power of the principles of Mind Mapping when applied to thinking. Leonardo's scientific notes are festooned with images, symbols, and associations. And what did Leonardo use these notes for? To become the greatest genius of all time, and the "best in the world" in his time, in physiology, anatomy, architecture, painting, aquanautics, aeronautics, astronomy, engineering, cooking, stringed musical instrument-playing, geology, and court-jesting, to name but a few!

Leonardo realized the power of using *images* and *associations* in order to unleash his brain's infinite capacity.

Follow his example! *Mind Map!*

your ideal future designed by

Mind Maps®

- Creating Your Ideal Future

- Mind Maps and the Future

- Computer Mind Maps

- A Dream Come True

Creating Your Ideal Future

You have now become aware of the extraordinary power of Mind Maps. One other major use for them is to help *you* to take control of *your* future!

You will probably already be aware of the fact that "you tend to get what you think you will get." A Mind Map, as the most sophisticated thinking tool in the world, can help you think very well about what you want. Such a Mind Map will therefore significantly increase the probability that you will get it!

Your next and exciting task is, therefore, to *let your imagination run riot*! Imagine that you have limitless time, resources and energy, and that you can do anything that you wish, for all eternity. Again, using a large sheet of blank paper, and having a compact image in the center that pictures, for you, the essence of your Ideal Future, develop a Mind Map (or ten!) on all those things you would like to accomplish if there were no limits placed upon you.

This Ideal Future Mind Map should include all those things you have dreamed, at any stage in your life, of doing. Some of the most common dreams include travel, learning new languages, learning to play a musical instrument, drawing and painting, writing, learning new dances, exploring new subjects, and taking up new mental and physical sports and activities. (One useful way to prepare your brain to do this Mind Map is to do a quick speed Mind Map on everything you do *not* want in your ideal future.)

Suggested topics for your main branches include: Skills; Education; Friends; Family; Job; Hobbies; and Goals. Mind Map the rest of your life exactly as you would design it if a genie from a magic lamp had said to you that if you Mind Mapped perfectly and extensively your ideal future, that genie would grant you every single wish!

When you are doing this Mind Map, make sure that you let your mind go totally, and Mind Map out everything you would truly like to do if you had that infinite time and money.

Include in this Mind Map as much color and as many images as you can in order to stimulate your creative thinking.

One other useful mini-Mind Map you can create while Mind Mapping your Ideal Future is an ideal *day* in your future. Using a clock as your central image, Mind Map all the major elements of that perfect day. After you have completed that Mind Map, make that perfect day every day of your real life.

When you have completed your Ideal Future Mind Map, use it as a stimulus and guide to add quality and hope to the **real** future that you are going to both live and create. Decide that you'll make as much of it as possible come true. Many people who have already tried this Mind Map have found it to be extraordinarily successful in transforming their lives and making them more happy and successful. Within a few years (or less!) of creating their Mind Maps, they have found that as much as 80% of their dreams have come true!

For an example of a completed Mind Map on this subject turn to Plate 8.

Mind Maps and the Future

What the brains of the world have needed is a thinking tool that reflects their natural ways of functioning—which allows them to use all the images and associations in the networking, radiant and explosive way to which they were born.

You are now in possession of that tool. The tool that one Irish broadcaster recently described as: "Perfect art for the mind."

The Mind Maps you make will amaze, delight, and enrich you.

Mind Maps will make your life more productive, fulfilled, and successful.

Mind Mapping is, in a very real sense, a co-operative *venture* and *adventure* between what we put on paper and what goes on in our heads.

You have already realized that Mind Maps can be used for as many different things as you can think about. And how many is that? Infinite!

In addition to the uses we have explored in this book, other popular uses for Mind Maps include:

- planning vacations, parties, weddings, events, jobs, and life;
- customer Mind Maps for salespeople, in which the growing relationship is constantly updated on the customer Mind Map;
- reviewing for study purposes;

- running and recording meetings;
- solving all sorts of problems including personal, interpersonal, and academic ones;
- getting perspectives on any situation;
- interviewing;
- running a household or multi-national business.

I leave you to explore the remaining infinite uses! If you come up with uses that you feel are really original, try them out, and let me know the result at my contact numbers on page 106.

A Dream Come True

When I invented Mind Maps, my original dream was to create a Master Thinking Tool that could be used easily by anybody, that could be applied to thousands of different situations and that would help people in all aspects of their lives; in other words, a tool that applied to life itself. This tool also had to enable the individual to express her- or himself uniquely—and very importantly, it had to be fun!

That tool turned out to be one that reflects the natural radiance and magnificence of your human brain. That tool was the Mind Map!

Mind Maps can help you in all daily activities, from the practical day-to-day level to the generation of important new ideas. Mind Maps are spreading around the world, and more and more people are adopting this profoundly useful thinking tool. I'm thrilled that you are now a member of this growing global community of Mind Mappers! I wish you continuing good fortune in the use of your amazing brain and its incredible thinking and Mind Mapping powers.

Index

Learning and Thinking for the 21st Century

- **Make the Most of Your Mind**
- **In-company Training**
- **Licensing for Companies and Independent Trainers**
- **"Open" Business and Public Seminars**
- **Educational Seminars**

We are the ONLY organization that can license use of the Mind Maps and associated trademarks

For full details of Buzan Learning Seminars and information on our range of BrainFriendly products, including:

- Books
- Software
- Audio and video tapes
- Support materials

SEND FOR OUR BROCHURE

Contact us at:

Email: Buzan@BuzanCentres.com

Website: www.Mind-Map.com

Or:

Buzan Centres Inc. (Americas)

PO Box 4, Palm Beach

Florida

FL33480, USA

Telephone: +1 561 881 0188

Fax: +1 561 434 1682

Buzan Centres Ltd (Rest of World)

54 Parkstone Road

Poole, Dorset BH15 2PG

Telephone: +44 (0) 1202 674676

Fax: +44 (0) 1202 674776

MAKE THE MOST OF YOUR MIND TODAY

Look out for *Mind Maps® for Kids*, available from February 2003.

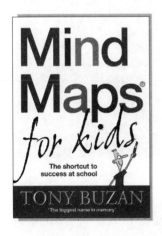

Help your children through their coursework and to exam success.

For more information on Tony Buzan or to download an extract, log on to **www.thorsons.com/buzan**.

Other titles by Tony Buzan published by Thorsons: